DATE DUE

MAY 2 7 2014	
FEB 1 7 2015	
JUN 0 6 2015	

BRODART, CO.   Cat. No. 23-221

ANCIENT INDIA
MAURYA
EMPIRE

JOHN BANKSTON

PUBLISHERS

P.O. Box 196
Hockessin, Delaware 19707
Visit us on the web: www.mitchelllane.com
Comments? email us: mitchelllane@mitchelllane.com

EXPLORE ANCIENT WORLDS

Ancient Assyria • Ancient Athens
The Aztecs • Ancient Babylon
The Byzantine Empire • The Celts of the British Isles
Ancient China • Ancient Egypt
Ancient India/Maurya Empire • Ancient Sparta

ABOUT THE AUTHOR: Born in Boston,
Massachusetts, John Bankston began writing
articles while still a teenager. Since then,
over two hundred of his articles have been
published in magazines and newspapers
across the country, including travel articles
in *The Tallahassee Democrat, The Orlando
Sentinel* and *The Tallahassean*. He is the author
of over sixty biographies for young adults,
including works on Alexander the Great,
scientist Stephen Hawking, author F. Scott
Fitzgerald and actor Jodi Foster. He currently
lives in Newport Beach, California.

PUBLISHER'S NOTE: The facts on which the story
in this book is based have been thoroughly
researched. Documentation of such research
can be found on page 45. While every
possible effort has been made to ensure
accuracy, the publisher will not assume liability
for damages caused by inaccuracies in the
data, and makes no warranty on the accuracy
of the information contained herein.

Printing   1   2   3   4   5   6   7   8   9

Library of Congress
Cataloging-in-Publication Data
Bankston, John, 1974-
 Ancient India/Maurya Empire / by John
Bankston.
    p. cm.
 Includes bibliographical references and index.
 ISBN 978-1-61228-280-0 (library bound)
 1. India—History—Maurya dynasty, ca. 322
B.C.-ca. 185 B.C.—Juvenile literature I. Title.
 DS425.B295 2013
 934'.04—dc23

                                    2012009409

eBook ISBN: 9781612283555

                                              PLB

CONTENTS

Chapter One
Civilization's Cradle 5
Sidebar: Indian Seals 11

Chapter Two
Cataclysm 13
Sidebar: Jainism and Buddhism 17

Chapter Three
Worldly Affairs 19
Sidebar: The *Arthashastra* 25

Chapter Four
Indika 27
Sidebar: Money 31

Chapter Five
Empire of Peace 33
Sidebar: Ashoka's Ruins 37

Ancient Craft: Terra Cotta 38

Ancient Recipes: Rice Pudding 40

Timeline 42

Chapter Notes 43

Works Consulted 45

Further Reading 46

Glossary 47

Index 48

Dhauligiri hills in Bhubaneswar, India, presumed to be the area where Kalinga War was fought by Ashoka.

Civilization's Cradle

Ashoka was horrified. Since becoming emperor of the Maurya Empire in about 270 BCE, he'd used his military forces to ruthlessly crush internal rebellions. He didn't anticipate anything different eight years later when he attacked Kalinga, his first invasion of a neighboring territory.

Kalinga was a small kingdom that stretched along the shores of the Bay of Bengal in eastern India. It was an independent country that could provide an important outlet to the sea for Ashoka's empire, which surrounded it on three sides. Before invading Kalinga, Ashoka had asked Kalinga's ruler to submit to his rule. The Kalingaraj refused.

Though they were out-armed and outnumbered, Kalingan warriors still mounted an impressive defense. Several times Ashoka declared victory, only to be attacked by fresh forces. After a conflict lasting about a year, the Mauryans' superior numbers prevailed.

No one knows how many people perished. Later in his reign, Ashoka constructed a number of edicts. These edicts contained proclamations of his ruling principles that were carved on highly polished stone pillars or massive rocks. They were placed in strategic points in his empire. One edict deals with Ashoka's own account of the Battle of Kalinga and its aftermath. According to Ashoka, over 10,000 Mauryan soldiers died. Among the Kalingans, the body count was far higher. At least 100,000 people lost their

Considered by many to be one of the greatest monarchs in history, Emperor Ashoka discouraged hunting and eating meat, eliminated many harsh punishments and promoted tolerance in the Maurya Empire.

lives. The dead were not just soldiers but also civilians, including women and children. More than 150,000 Kalingans were deported.

Ashoka was no stranger to violence. According to many reports, he killed some of his brothers, who had been rivals to his claim to the throne of the Maurya Empire. He may also have established prisons in which the inmates were horribly tortured. Yet he was sickened by the extent of the violence and destruction he had caused in Kalinga. After listing the casualty figures on the edict, Ashoka confessed that he "... felt remorse, for, when an independent country is conquered the slaughter, death, and deportation of the people is extremely grievous [damaging]...and weighs heavily on [my] mind…any sons or great grandsons that I may have should not think of gaining new conquests."[1]

As a result of the slaughter, Ashoka was profoundly changed. He took his own advice, and stopped trying to expand his territory, like his grandfather—who had founded the empire more than half a century

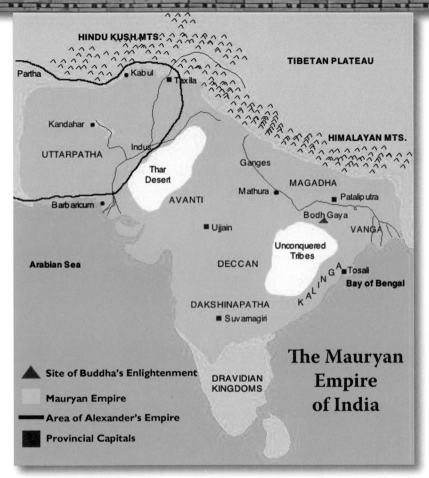

The Mauryan
Empire
of India

Site of Buddha's Enlightenment

Mauryan Empire

Area of Alexander's Empire

Provincial Capitals

earlier—or his father had done. Instead, for the rest of his reign, he devoted himself to spreading peace.

It was not an easy task. At its peak, Ashoka's empire sprawled across most of what today is known as the Indian subcontinent. Besides modern-day India, it includes the nations of Afghanistan, Bangladesh, Nepal, Pakistan, Sri Lanka and Tibet. It covers over 1,700,000 square miles, or about two and a half percent of the Earth's surface, while containing about a sixth of the world's population.

The first inhabitants had arrived in the region from northern Asia and Africa many thousands of years ago. They were nomadic, traveling by foot for hundreds of miles. Those in central and northern India made their way through the Khyber Pass, a path cutting through the Hindu Kush mountain range. They were hunter-gatherers who followed the food and rarely stayed in one place for very long. Surviving on various plants including nuts and berries, they hunted whatever animals did not hunt them. It was a difficult, brutal existence.

Slowly, some nine thousand years ago, that changed. Near the Bolan River in the western part of modern-day Pakistan, some of them settled down, cultivated wheat and other crops, and began domesticating animals in a community named Mehrgarh, which lasted for nearly five thousand years. At about the same time, several distinct civilizations began developing in other parts of the world: the Egyptians in North Africa, the Mayans in South America, the Chinese, and the Sumerians in modern-day Iraq. They had one thing in common. All were close to the Tropic of Cancer. This location offers consistent mild weather because the sun remains high in the

This early farming village in Mehrgarh, c. 7000 BCE, shows houses built with mud bricks.

Early hunter-gatherers often survived by eating plants like the wild barley shown here. Learning to grow their own food allowed people to develop societies.

sky for much of the year. The result is a long growing season, which was vital for early farmers. Fertile soil and abundant rainfall meant these early settlers were not as worried about starvation as nomads were.

Around 3200 BCE, villages began developing along the Indus River. With a length of about 1800 miles, it is one of the longest on Earth. India was named for it, though today it flows through Pakistan.

Although earlier humans had used stone tools, in the Indus Valley villages smelting was being developed. This process of turning mineral ores such as copper or bronze into metal produced weapons and tools like the plow, which apparently began being utilized in the Indus Valley between 3000 and 2500 BCE.

Villagers no longer needed to spend most of their waking hours searching for food. Now they could turn their attention to constructing cities and enacting laws. They developed a written language, which was carved onto seals.

Harappa

In 1826, a British army deserter named James Lewis discovered an ancient village. Writing as Charles Masson sixteen years later, he described how behind his camp lay a "ruinous brick castle...The walls and towers of the castle are remarkably high, though, from having been long deserted, they exhibit in some parts the ravages of time and decay...Tradition affirms the existence here of a city."[2] It was called Harappa.

Archaeologists, people who study the remains of earlier cultures—everything from bones to pottery—began uncovering other ruins in the same area. One of the most notable was called Mohenjo-Daro. Archaeologists soon came to believe that these were the oldest planned cities in the world. Though separated by nearly 400 miles, Mohenjo-Daro and Harappa are nearly identical. Both feature low-lying homes of brick and stone built along streets laid down in grid patterns. Most houses had bathrooms, and channels carved into the streets provided a place for sewage to flow out. It was one of the earliest known public sanitation systems, predating the ones in Rome by more than two thousand years.

Mohenjo-Daro, Harappa and similar cities welcomed merchants from other parts of the Asian continent. Trade flourished. To ensure fairness, the Indus Valley people developed a system of weights and measures. At its peak, it was the most sophisticated culture on earth. And it was about to be destroyed.

Indian Seals

Sir Alexander Cunningham is considered the father of Indian archaeology. An English officer assigned to the Bengal Engineers, he used the writings of two Chinese monks who had visited India over one thousand years earlier as a guide and uncovered a number of important sites.

A Harappan unicorn seal, dated 2400 BC

In May of 1870, Cunningham was appointed the director-general of the Archaeological Survey of India. Two years later, he discovered a seal with the image of a unicorn at the city of Harappa. In 1875, he wrote about a seal he'd linked to the Indus Valley civilization.

Since then, hundreds of the two-inch seals have been unearthed and linked to the ancient culture. Often carved onto soapstone, they have images of antelopes, tigers, crocodiles and rhinoceroses. Most also have characters, like the letters of an alphabet which appear to have formed words. They have never been translated.

Many seals were pressed into clay, then stuck to goods that would be sold. They might have given information about the seller or the product. Other seals seem to show gods or religious images. This is interesting since little is known about the religion of the Indus Valley civilization.

Seals connected to the Maurya Empire have also been discovered. Often made of bone, ivory or terra cotta (a type of clay) they usually included the name of the owner or were issued by royalty. These seals have been translated and help historians form an impression of the Maurya Empire.

Ganges River at Rishikesh

CHAPTER 2

Cataclysm

Brick houses lined the streets. Art and literature blossomed. And then the civilization disappeared, buried beneath tons of shifting sand.

In the 19th century, Asian language scholar Max Müller suggested that the society was destroyed by invaders. Recently, this view has been questioned.

The society's decline took centuries. Yet it may have begun with a single cataclysm. Some historians suggest that a volcanic eruption around 1900 BCE led to the Indus Valley society's downfall. Even from thousands of miles away, the ash and smoke pouring into the atmosphere would have reduced sunlight and altered the growing seasons.

Another theory is that a large earthquake affected the smaller rivers fed by the Indus. Ancient settlements east of the Indus were discovered buried beneath many feet of sand. Surrounded by the Thar Desert, these communities could not have survived in such dry conditions. They must have had a reliable source of water. The land must have been fertile.

Shifting rivers, or even ones that disappeared entirely, may have hastened the decline.

Flooding is still another possibility. It would have destroyed crops and upset the delicate balance of the Indus Valley society. Some people moved on, settling by the Ganges River in northwestern India.

As crops failed, the once-peaceful society was torn apart. By about 1500 BCE, it had almost completely disappeared. The only remnants were squatters who huddled in the ruins of the onetime planned communities.

At about the same time, a nomadic tribe from Central Asia descended onto the Indus Valley. They were called the Aryans. They did not cultivate crops. They could not read or write. Their arrival may have been less an invasion than an opportunity. Professor Jonathan Mark Kenoyer notes, "Episodes of aggression and conflict probably occurred, but armed conflict was not a major activity."[1]

Without a war, without an invasion, there probably was an assimilation. The Aryans entering India learned from the natives. Many people who had lived in the area fled south (where today they represent a distinct group), but those remaining may have helped the Aryans. Once they had settled, Aryans followed Indian practices of crop rotation—growing different crops each season. This technique is used by modern farmers.

Unlike their predecessors, the Aryans left little of their actual civilization behind. There are no ruins of ancient Aryan towns. Their heritage is something else, as their arrival coincides with the four Vedas. Written in the Sanskrit language starting around 1500 BCE and continuing for several centuries, the Vedas are considered the oldest sacred texts in the world. Veda means "to know." Knowing the four Vedas helps to understand how the people lived. It is also a beginning to understanding the Hindu religion.

Today Hinduism is India's dominant religion. Hinduism eventually replaced the original Aryan gods with such now-familiar deities as Brahma, who created the universe; Vishnu, the supreme god; and Shiva, the transforming god. The religion views life as a struggle between good and evil. All choices have consequences, or karma. Each person's religious path—their dharma—is based on their social class. The Aryans created a caste system, which became even more defined as Hinduism evolved.

In this system, the Brahmans composed the highest level of society. They were the priests, who knew the sacred texts, performed religious rites, and earned the best treatment. On the other hand, they had the strictest rules for conduct because they were expected to attain the highest levels of

The warrior nobles called
Kshatriyas

purity. For example, they couldn't come in contact with dirt. Then came the Kshatriyas, or warriors. This caste was composed of the kings and other rulers, as well as the fighters who helped them maintain their high positions. They protected the society from dangers.

Third were the Vaishyas, or cultivators. This caste consisted of merchants, artisans, traders, and landowners who engaged in agriculture and raising cattle. The lowest were Shudras, or servants, many of whom were native Indians. Their role was to serve the three higher castes. They performed menial tasks, often doing work that no one else wanted to.

Eventually another group evolved, the Harijans, or untouchables—a name Indians took literally. Because they did "dirty work," they had to live apart from other Indians and were considered outcasts.

"The social caste to which a person belonged determined their role in life, their employment and their dharma," explains the book *India*.[2] Eventually the system became very specialized, with literally thousands of sub-castes.

This stupa marks the spot where the Buddha beheld the
Magadha Empire and taught law for seven consecutive days.

Over time, the Aryan civilization began developing into increasingly larger towns, which in turn developed into even larger kingdoms. By the sixth century BCE, Indian history becomes more defined. By that time, there were sixteen major states in northern India. The most important was the kingdom of Magadha, located in the northeastern part of the Indian subcontinent. It began expanding in the middle of the sixth century BCE under the leadership of Bimbisara. At about the same time, two important religions—Jainism and Buddhism—were founded in Magadha. A little over a century later, Mahapadma Nanda came to power and founded a dynasty bearing his name that lasted for a century. Including land west from Punjab to Bengal to south of the Decca Plateau, the kingdom also briefly included the Kalinga Empire. The rulers imposed huge, unpopular taxes, hastening their eventual downfall.

In 518 BCE, King Darius I of Persia invaded the Indus Valley, which altered the area's politics and culture while leaving it vulnerable to outside invasion. For over a century, the region suffered minor conflicts, until one of the world's greatest military leaders paved the way for the Maurya Empire.

Jainism and Buddhism

Hindu's rigid caste system is one reason why two new religions, Jainism and Buddhism, originated in the 500s BCE. Neither confines individuals to a single place in society.

Of Jainism's 24 spiritual leaders, the main one is a former prince named Vardhamana. Born

Buddha

about 540 BCE, at age 30 he became an ascetic. A Jain ascetic does not wear any clothing or own material things. He lives a life of non-violence. Since Jains believe animals and plants have souls just as people do, they try not to harm any living thing and become vegetarians. After thirteen years, Vardhamana achieved enlightenment and earned the title of "Great Hero," or Mahavira.

Buddhism's spiritual leader also went through a profound change as an adult. Born into a royal family around 560 BCE, Siddhartha Gautama enjoyed great luxury. As an adult, he also became an ascetic. Soon, however, he said, "These so-called austerities only confuse the mind, which is overpowered by later exhaustion."[3]

After 49 days of meditation, he reached enlightenment. From the age of 35, he was the Buddha, or "Awakened One." Until his death in his eighties, he spread Buddhism's core message: Life is suffering, suffering comes from cravings, and release from suffering comes from those who follow the noble eightfold path of Buddhism.

The religion reached its peak of popularity in India two centuries after Buddha's death. Today millions of Indians are practicing Buddhists, and it has many more millions of believers around the world.

German painter Albrecht Altdorfer's 1529 painting *The Battle of Alexander at Issus* depicts the great conqueror's victory over the Persian army in 333 BCE.

CHAPTER 3

Worldly Affairs

Many authorities consider Alexander the Great to be the world's most successful military leader. Born in 356 BCE in the Greek region of Macedonia, he succeeded his father Philip II as king when he was just 22. Soon afterward, Alexander began one of the most brilliant military campaigns of all time, conquering the Persian Empire and establishing his authority over more than two million square miles of land.

Alexander's soldiers crossed the Indus River and entered India in the spring of 326 BCE. They quickly conquered Taxila and Punjab. Alexander's next goal was the kingdom of Magadha. But when his army reached the Beas River, which lay between them and Magadha, his troops rebelled. Exhausted, homesick, and discouraged by heavy losses during the fighting in India, the soldiers refused to march any further. Alexander soon withdrew from India. Despite the setback, Alexander learned from the Indians. Like them, he began using elephants in military campaigns. His Greek scientists shared their knowledge of philosophy and medicine with the natives. Indian astronomers revealed their own discoveries.

Three years after leaving India, Alexander died. The warrior who had survived dozens of battles apparently lost his life to food poisoning. His empire splintered into several smaller kingdoms. One of Alexander's generals, Seleucus Nicator, received the easternmost area, which included

India. But Seleucus became involved in a struggle for other parts of Alexander's empire and ignored India.

While he was still in India, Alexander inspired an Indian teenager who shared his dreams of conquest. But instead of invading distant lands, Chandragupta Maurya envisioned a united India, especially under the uncertain and confused conditions that existed with the withdrawal of Greek influence.

Historical documents offer few details about Chandragupta's life. His birth is tentatively put at sometime around 340 BCE. Some Buddhist writings suggest Chandragupta's mother was a maidservant, while his father may have been a village chief or perhaps even a son of the Nanda dynasty king Sarvarthasiddhi. Many scholars believe that he grew up, not

This Indian stamp honors Chandragupta Maurya, the founder of the Maurya Empire.

Peacocks remain the national bird of India

in great wealth, but rather in a village of men who tamed peacocks, or mayuras. These colorful birds gave their name to the empire that Chandragupta would found.

Assisted by a Taxilian Brahman named Kautilya, Chandragupta rose from his humble background and assembled what some people insultingly called a band of thieves and soldiers for hire. He set his sights on Punjab, a region already weakened by Alexander's invasion. Its subjects were sick of enduring the Macedonian occupation.

Historians aren't sure when Chandragupta attacked, though it probably came between 324 and 320 BCE. Leading his supposedly motley army, he drove out the foreign occupiers. His stunning success brought alliances, as other leaders who were impressed by his initial successes wanted to join him. Moving east, the growing army invaded Magadha.

At the city of Pataliputra a decisive battle raged. The assault was bloody. After winning the battle, Chandragupta ordered his men to execute King

Dhana Nanda and everyone related to him. The city became the capital of Chandragupta's Maurya Empire.

Within a few years the empire stretched across most of the Indian subcontinent. But by then Selecus had settled his issues with his fellow generals. Attacking India in 305 BCE, he wanted to reestablish the control Alexander had had two decades earlier. Instead, he encountered Chandragupta's now-massive army, which may have included 9,000 war elephants. It's not clear if the two armies actually fought, but it soon became apparent to Seleucus that he had no hope of winning. He decided to bargain with Chandragupta. For the price of 500 war elephants, Seleucus gave Chandragupta the land where Afghanistan now lies. That territory included India's natural western border, the Hindu Kush mountain range. He apparently also gave Chandragupta one of his daughters, who married either the emperor himself or one of his sons.

War elephants

Alexander the Great was considered the world's best general. By the time he was thirty, his army had conquered Persia, Greece and Egypt. He was one of the richest men in the world.

While Alexander remains by far the more famous of the two men, Chandragupta can boast of one accomplishment that eluded the Greek. He had not only retaken all the land that Alexander had conquered, he added even more—thereby uniting virtually all of India as a single empire.

This empire was described as "the largest and most rigorously administered kingdom in Ancient India."[1] Much of what we know about how the Maurya Empire was run comes from a book called the *Arthashastra*. According to noted historian and filmmaker Michael Wood, "the central idea of the work is the artha (prosperity) of a kingdom—how to get it and how to keep it."[2]

Along with accounts by foreign ambassadors and numerous Buddhist writings, this work provides the knowledge that French scholar Alain Daniélou suggests is when "India enters history in terms of the meaning we

The *Arthashastra*

give to the word. Starting from this time we possess important original documents, written by Indians and foreigners...in languages we can read and understand with certitude."[3]

Despite existing over two thousand years ago, some of the Maurya Empire's rules and regulations are familiar to 21st century readers. The *Arthashastra* describes a series of consumer protections regulating the buying and selling of goods. There are laws protecting patients from doctors who may harm them. There were rules related to the treatment of workers, and a system of measurements ensuring that trade in goods was uniform (just as a quart of milk means the same thing in New York as it does in California).

A chapter on the duties of the Superintendent of Weights and Measures explains that "Weights (*pratimánáni*) shall be made of iron or of stones available in the countries of Magadha and Mekala; or of such things as will neither contract when wetted, nor expand under the influence of heat."[4] An appropriate scale should feature a "wooden balance with a lever eight hands long, with measuring marks and counterpoise weights [and it] shall be erected on a pedestal like that of a peacock."[5]

As Chandragupta's closest advisor and the credited author of the *Arthashastra,* Kautilya helped him run an empire. What he could not predict was the way religion would change both the country's leader and the country itself.

The *Arthashastra*

Rudrapatnam Shamashastry

When Indian scholar Rudrapatnam Shamashastry looked at the manuscript of the *Arthashastra* he had been given in 1905, he knew it was over one hundred years old. He was right about the age of the manuscript. The words it contained, however, were much, much older. Written for a king in the Sanskrit language, it opens with "Om," the most sacred syllable in Hinduism and Buddhism. The work explained "this Arthashastra had been prepared mostly by bringing together the teaching of many treatises [formal works on a topic] composed by ancient teachers for the acquisition and protection of the earth."[6] Describing the topics the reader would encounter, it "asserted that this work, easy to learn and understand, and marked by precision in ideas, word, and meaning, had been composed by Kautilya."[7]

Although Kautilya, Chandragupta's chief minister, is credited as the author, some historians believe others wrote at least some of its parts. The *Arthashastra* is sometimes compared to a 16th century Italian work, Niccolò Machiavelli's *The Prince*. It claimed that achieving a ruler's goals—like glory or survival—can justify doing bad things.

The *Arthashastra* describes a government that oversees nearly every action of its subjects. It does not reflect the exact workings of the empire. Instead it's an ideal—the way the writer (or writers) believed a country should be run, not the way it actually was. Still, it gives modern-day readers a taste of what life was like in the Maurya Empire.

An example of an Indian wooden palace
(Padmanabapuram palace)

The streets of Pataliputra were filled with marketplaces and racetracks, inns and gambling halls. Many houses had bathrooms with drain pipes; beside them, round stone pillars offered protection from the errant wheels of carts and chariots. The capital itself was protected by a high wall nearly ten miles long, hundreds of towers for archers, and an encircling moat. Located at the junction of the Ganges and Son Rivers, it may have been the largest city in the world.

Emperor Chandragupta's palace stood as a symbol of his success. Silver and gold plating adorned the walls, while the grounds were landscaped and featured fish ponds and tame animals. Parrots chattered while peacocks displayed their colorful plumage.

The emperor was entertained by slave women. As one account noted, "The care of the king's person is entrusted to women, who also are bought from their parents. The guards and the rest of the soldiery attend outside the gates.

"The king leaves his palace not only in time of war, but also for the purpose of judging causes....Crowds of women surround him, and outside of this circle spearmen are ranged. The road is marked off with ropes, and it is death, for man and woman alike, to pass within the ropes....Of the women, some are in chariots, some on horses, and some even on elephants, and they are equipped with weapons of every kind, as if they were going on a campaign."[1]

The castle and the two-story homes which filled the city had one thing in common. They were constructed of wood. Unlike the stone structures of the earlier Indus Valley society, most of Pataliputra's buildings did not last.

What did last were words. The best accounts of life during the period of the Maurya Empire came from outsiders. Greek ambassador Megasthenes began living in the capital in 302 BCE while representing the interests of Seleucus. Writing down his observations in a book entitled *Indika,* he offered a detailed account of an empire few people had visited. The work as a whole has disappeared, but fragments endure.

Questions about *Indika's* accuracy arose soon after it was written. "India was opened up to our knowledge," wrote Pliny the Younger, "by other Greek writers, who having resided with Indian kings—as for instance

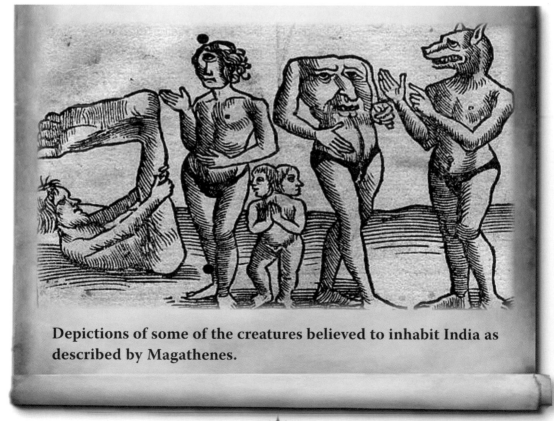

Depictions of some of the creatures believed to inhabit India as described by Magathenes.

Megasthenes... made known the strength of the peoples of the country. It is not, however, worthwhile to study their accounts with care, so conflicting are they, and incredible."[2]

But alongside *Indika's* fantastic descriptions of ants digging for gold and men with ears so large that people can sleep in them are realistic passages about life in the empire. Describing the Mauryans, Megasthenes wrote that they, "having abundant means of subsistence, exceed in consequence the ordinary stature, and are distinguished by their proud bearing. They are also found to be well-skilled in the arts, as might be expected of men who inhale a pure air and drink the very finest water."[3]

Older cities grew. Trade increased. Specialized crafts, like iron and copper making, attracted numerous buyers. Universities were established while trade guilds provided an education in the crafts. The empire collected taxes but it did not own the land. Individuals worked on their own property. The government also issued money, widely used in the cities. Rural areas often used a barter system, in which goods and services were traded for each other.

The Maurya Empire was male-dominated. Men made the rules. Men had the power. Although they protected the emperor, and hunted as equals, women could be married when they turned twelve, often to men they did not like. If a woman brought money into the marriage—a dowry—and her husband died, the dowry went to her son.

If a woman did not obey her husband, the *Arthashastra* said she could be punished by "three beats either with a bamboo-bark or with a rope or with the palm of the hand may be given on her hips."[4] If she could not have children, or only had daughters, the husband could marry another because "women are created for the sake of sons."[5]

Still, women enjoyed legal protections denied to women in many cultures even today. Women who did not have sons could keep their dowry after the husband's death. "If a husband either is of bad character or is long gone abroad," wrote the *Arthashastra,* "or has become a traitor to his king or is likely to endanger the life of his wife or has fallen from his caste or has lost virility, he may be abandoned by his wife."[6]

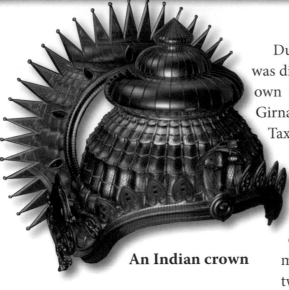

An Indian crown

During Chandragupta's reign, the empire was divided into five provinces, each with its own capital. In Kathiawar, the capital was Girnar; the Northwest frontier's capital was Taxila; Ujjain was the capital of Central India, while the Gulf of Bengal's capital was Tosali, and the south was run from the capital of Suvarnagiri.

The *Arthashastra* outlines the role of eight ministers. Later accounts mention twelve, sixteen and even twenty. In the Maurya Empire, food production was vital, so the most important post was minister of agriculture. Others mentioned in the *Arthashastra* include the ministers of prisons, treasury, revenue and armies.

Other accounts agree with its opinion that ministers should be encouraged to disagree with their king. "Sovereignty (*rájatva*) is possible only with assistance," it notes in a chapter entitled "The Life of a Saintly King." "A single wheel can never move. Hence he shall employ ministers and hear their opinion."[7]

The document never anticipated the impact of a ruler's religious conversion. The Hindu religion and its caste system were dominant. Most accounts suggest Chandragupta was born into a lower caste.

Chandragupta converted to Jainism, which was more accepting of his background. Around the year 297 BCE, he abdicated—stepping down from the throne and allowing his son Bindusara to rule. Then he ended his life according to the ideals of his religion. As a Jain monk, he kept its tradition of *vanaprastha,* or "return to the forest." He fasted—he stopped eating. Despite his great wealth, Chandragupta died just as many poor people did. He starved to death.

Money

Chandragupta's palace decayed, leaving just a few stone columns. Cities crumbled, and only paving stones and drainpipes survived. Over two thousand years later, archeologists found terra cotta ornaments along with children's toys, pots, and cookware. Still, money probably symbolized the Maurya Empire's organization and wealth more than other discoveries.

Alexander coin

Beginning in the early 1800s, British official James Tod encouraged Indians to collect coins unearthed by torrential rains. In 1924, over 1,000 silver and gold coins issued by Alexander the Great were discovered in Taxila. They connected the modern world to the lives lived thousands of years ago.

The *Arthashastra* offered detailed instructions for minting, or producing, money. Silver coins were worth 16 times what a copper coin was worth. The coins were decorated with elephants and hills. The bird which gave the empire its name is well represented, as many of the coins discovered from that era feature peacocks.

Coins had once been different from region to region (as if both New England and the Pacific Northwest produced their own currency). Under the Mauryans, however, money became more uniform. The coins were either round or square and they always had five punch marks. The sun was always seen as one of the punches, so too was a six-armed symbol. The marks also allowed money changers to know where the coins had been minted.

Farmlands of India

CHAPTER
5

Empire of Peace

By the time of his abdication, Emperor Chandragupta had radically altered his country. He'd expanded its borders and improved his subjects' lives. Well-cultivated farmland produced an abundance of food; merchants traveled hundreds of miles to trade within its borders. His son Bindusara inherited a stable kingdom.

Bindusara's reign was less about conquest than consolidation. He crushed rebellions and kept the kingdom united.

Bindusara had numerous wives, at least 16 according to some accounts. As a result, he also had many sons. He treated one worse than all the others. Some accounts suggest this was because he thought the boy was ugly.

Bindusara still listened to his father's advisor. Kautilya suggested the emperor send this least-favorite son to crush a rebellion in Taxila. The prince was just a teenager when he accompanied the chief minister to the Northwest frontier. At the capital, the emperor's son learned that the city supported his father's rule. They only opposed the local leaders' cruelty.

The prince ended the rebellion without bloodshed. He would not always be so lucky. His mother had named him Ashoka, which means "I am without sorrow." It was more hope than prophecy. The young prince would soon know great sorrow—a sorrow which would change both his life and his country's future.

Becoming emperor was brutal. Following Bindusara's death in 273 BCE, Ashoka battled his brothers to ascend to the throne. One legend claims he killed 99 of them. The Buddhist text *Ashokavadana* says he "managed to become king after getting rid of the legitimate heir, by tricking him into entering a pit filled with live coals."[1]

Once he was emperor, Ashoka fought just as hard to preserve the kingdom he'd inherited.

The prisons filled with those who opposed him. Ashoka's men tortured some and executed others. "He became notorious as 'Ashoka the Fierce,'" notes one history, "because of his wicked nature and bad temper. He submitted his ministers to a test of loyalty and had 500 of them killed because he found them wanting."[2] He built "an elaborate and horrific torture chamber, where he amused himself by watching the agony of his unfortunate victims."[3]

For the first eight years of his reign, he battled against rebelling provinces. Then his attention turned to expansion.

Kalinga had been part of the Magadha Empire. It gained independence when Ashoka's grandfather became emperor. Ashoka's father conquered adjoining Andhra. Invading Kalinga probably seemed like a natural progression for Ashoka.

The battle changed him. Despite winning the conflict, he was profoundly affected by the slaughter. Ashoka turned from war toward peace. A Buddhist teacher named Upagupta of Mathura converted him to the religion.

The emperor led by example. As a Buddhist, he stopped eating meat. As a vegetarian, he stopped hunting.

"Formerly in the kitchens [of Emperor Ashoka] many hundreds of thousands of living animals were killed daily for meat," he wrote in the first of many stone edicts he erected throughout the kingdom. "But now at the time of this writing... only three animals are killed... Even these three animals will not be killed in the future."[4]

He avoided using the royal treasury to buy luxuries. Instead of living in the palace, he spent much of the year visiting other provinces. Traveling across the empire, Ashoka spread his message of peace. He supported

The Dambulla cave temples in Sri Lanka date back to the 1st century BCE.

Buddhist missionaries who talked about the religion across the country. He even sent his son to Ceylon. Today, as the country of Sri Lanka, it is still a primary location for Buddhism in the region.

Despite encouraging his subjects to convert to Buddhism, he accepted other religions and did not punish those who worshipped differently. In his seventh edict, Ashoka wrote that he "already desireth that all unbelievers may be brought to repentance and peace of mind. He is anxious that every diversity of opinion, and every diversity of passion, may shine forth blended into one system, and be conspicuous in undistinguishing charity."[5]

Indeed, while Buddhism never became India's dominant religion, many of its ideals were "blended" into Hinduism. Ashoka did not just try to end the harming of animals. A few histories suggest he stopped harming people as well.

In *Indika,* Megasthenes described how during the reign of Chandragupta lawbreakers were harshly punished. "A person convicted of bearing false witness suffers mutilation of his extremities," he wrote. "He who maims any one not only suffers in return the loss of the same limb, but his hand also is cut off. If he causes an artisan [skilled craftsman] to lose his hand or his eye, he is put to death."[6]

Ashoka ended that practice. He opened free hospitals and veterinary clinics. He oversaw the planting of thousands of trees. He supervised the design of thousands of stupas, the dome shrines to Buddha.

He ended the bloody conquests of his grandfather's reign. Unfortunately, his focus on Buddhism and peace made Ashoka vulnerable. One Buddhist account claims that his ministers stopped him from giving away money from the royal treasury. "Ashoka then started giving away his own personal possessions," explains one history. "Finally he was left with only one [piece of fruit] which too he gifted."[7]

Others claim that Ashoka's grandson Samprati ended his rule. With the support of his father's ministers, Samprati (who later became emperor himself) confined Ashoka to the palace and fed him barely enough to survive.

There are only limited accounts of the emperors who ruled after Ashoka died, probably in 232 BCE. None lasted very long. Attacked by warring neighbors and torn apart by rebelling provinces, the Maurya Empire slowly split apart. Sometime around 184 BCE, the last emperor, Brihadratha, was murdered by Pushyamitra, his chief military advisor. Pushyamitra founded the Shunga dynasty.

Ashoka

Today many Indians consider Ashoka to be ancient India's greatest emperor. His admirers aren't limited to Indians. Nineteenth century historian and science fiction author H.G. Wells (famous for books like *War of the Worlds, The Invisible Man: A Grotesque Romance,* and *The Time Machine*) wrote, "Amidst the tens of thousands of names of monarchs that crowd the columns of history...the name of Ashoka shines, and shines almost alone, a star."[8]

The legacy of the Maurya Empire and Emperor Ashoka endures. To celebrate the site where Buddha first taught the Dharma, the emperor erected a pillar that featured four lions standing back-to-back. When India became a republic on January 26, 1950, the new nation adopted the Ashokan lions as its emblem. The four regal cats stand for courage, power, pride and confidence.

In the center of India's flag sits a blue wheel with 24 spokes. This Buddhist "Wheel of Law" is known as Ashoka's Chakra. Representing the nation's continuing progress, it symbolizes the importance of justice in life.

Ashoka's Ruins

While many earlier symbols of the Maurya Empire crumbled, Ashoka's memory is preserved in the pillars and rocks where he wrote his edicts. He is said to have constructed 80,000 of these monuments.

Ashoka pillar

Europeans began discovering Ashoka's pillars and stones in the 1500s. It was not until the early 1800s that they began understanding what was written upon them. In 1837, British official James Prinsep realized the writing on Ashoka's pillars matched what he'd seen on a stupa elsewhere. He noticed the same word was repeated in each line. It probably meant "donate" or "give" and guessed it was lists of people who'd donated money to build the stupa. Working from that clue, Prinsep eventually translated Ashoka's pillars.

Today one of the best preserved Mauryan artifacts is the Great Stupa in Sanchi. Like many others, it features four lions joined at the back and the Dharma Chakra.

The decline of Buddhism in India led to the stupa's decline. The lack of use was beneficial, however, when Muslim armies destroyed numerous active temples—both Buddhist and Hindi—following an invasion centuries later.

Today many surviving remnants of the Maurya Empire are outside India. Some of Ashoka's edicts are in Afghanistan, while many stupas are in Pakistan. Because of conflicts relating to the Afghanistan war, visiting such sites is dangerous. Fortunately, a number of artifacts from the Maurya Empire have been collected in museums, both in India and around the world.

Ancient Craft: Terra Cotta

The ancient Indians used terra cotta to make everything from toys and beads to vessels and idols for worship. Terra cotta is Latin for "baked earth." Usually made from river clay, it is either baked in the sun or a kiln.

Today during festival times, Indians use terra cotta to make gods to pray to and toys to play with. Festivities often end with the release of terra cotta gods into the river. Sending terra cotta creations back to the river from where they came reflects, in a way, the cycle of birth and rebirth familiar in Hindu culture.

Terra cotta is inexpensive and fun to work with. Terra cotta "oven-bake" clay can be purchased at most hobby or arts and crafts stores. This clay just requires a regular oven to "cook," rather than a pottery kiln.

There are many terra cotta items you can make: seals, toys such as animals, sculptures and much more. You can look at pictures of seals discovered in the Indus Valley or Maurya cultures. Or you can create your own. Most seals are about two inches by two inches.

MATERIALS

- Terra Cotta "oven-bake" clay
- Roller (either baking or non-stick)
- Acrylic paint (preferably that cleans with soap and water)
- Metal cutouts such as stars and hearts
- Plastic terra cotta tools

DIRECTIONS

1. Wash your hands and start with a clean surface.
2. Knead a handful of clay with the roller until it is flat and smooth.
3. Craft your designs on a cookie sheet or similar surface, to eliminate the challenge of transferring a design from one place to another. Use your cutouts to create existing shapes or your tools to design new ones. For larger shapes, like the terra cotta dogs found in the Indus Valley, use crumpled aluminum foil as the "skeleton."
4. Place the cookie sheet with your designs in an oven (though not a microwave) set at 275 degrees Fahrenheit. Cook for fifteen minutes per 1/4 inch of thickness. Be careful not to overcook.
5. Remove the sheet from the oven and let the designs cool for an hour.
6. When the terra cotta is cool, apply the paint.

Ancient Recipe: Rice Pudding

When Indians want to celebrate, they collect the choicest fruits of their labor—fragrant rice, fresh creamy milk and butter from their beloved cows, nuts, spices—sweeten it with molasses from sugar cane, and cook it on a low flame. Kheer (as it is known in the North) and payasam (in the South) varies only in consistency, flavorings, and sweeteners. Rice, milk, and butter compose the unchanging base to which the rest is added.

Prep time - 15 minutes
Cook time - 45 minutes
Serves 4

INGREDIENTS
½ cup Basmati rice
2 cups full cream milk
2 cups water
4 oz condensed sweetened milk
sugar to taste
2 tablespoons unsalted butter or ghee (clarified butter)
2 tablespoons almond slices
2 tablespoons green raisons
2 pods green cardamom

EQUIPMENT NEEDED
Can opener
Mortar and pestle/spice grinder
Saucepan
Sauté pan

PREPARATION

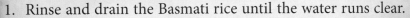

1. Rinse and drain the Basmati rice until the water runs clear.
2. Pour the milk and water into a heavy bottomed saucepan. Add the Basmati. Bring to a boil. Reduce the flame to medium and keep stirring every now and then to prevent the mixture from boiling over or burning. Cook until the Basmati turns thick and mushy.
3. While the rice is cooking, heat 1 tablespoon of butter in a sauté pan and brown the almonds and then the raisins. Set aside.
4. Grind the green cardamom in the spice grinder with a teaspoon of granulated sugar. Optionally, pound in the mortar till all the little black seeds are crushed and discard the green outer shell.
5. When the rice is done, add the condensed milk. Taste for sweetness. Add sugar to taste if needed.
6. Take the pudding off the stove and add the crushed cardamom and sautéed almonds and raisins. Top with the remaining butter. Mix well.
7. Serve hot or cold, either by itself or with fresh tropical fruit like sliced mangoes, pineapples, bananas.

All dates BCE

ca 7000	Nomadic hunters settle along the Bolan River in what is now Pakistan and begin farming and domesticating animals.
ca 3200	In the Indus Valley, early Indians begin crafting metal tools using copper, bronze and later iron.
3000	Settlements are built in Southern India. Geography will shelter the region from the kinds of invasions endured by the North.
ca 1900	Agriculture begins declining in the Indus Valley.
1500	With its cities weak and impoverished, the residents of the Indus Valley are overcome by Aryans from Central Asia.
ca 1500	The first Vedas are composed.
ca 1000	Aryans begin using iron implements.
ca 550	Jainism is founded by Mahavira.
ca 520	Buddhism is founded after former Prince Siddhartha Gautama achieves enlightenment.
518	King Darius I of Persia invades western Indus Valley.
326	Alexander the Great invades India, but his exhausted troops refuse to cross the Beas River and he retreats.
ca 320	Chandragupta Maurya begins fight to consolidate the Maurya Empire.
305	Chandragupta defeats Seleucus's effort to restore Greek rule to western India and rules over the largest empire in ancient India.
304	Possible birth of Ashoka, according to some sources.
ca 300	Kautilya, chief minister of the Maurya Empire, writes the *Arthashastra*.
297	Chandragupta Maurya steps down from the throne and soon fasts to death; his son Bindusara succeeds him as emperor.
273	Bindusara dies.
ca 268	Ashoka becomes emperor after several years of bloody and deadly fighting with his brothers
261	Ashoka wins the Battle of Kalinga, and undergoes conversion soon afterward.
232	Ashoka dies.
232-224	Reign of Emperor Dasharatha.*
224-215	Reign of Emperor Samprati.*
215-202	Reign of Emperor Shalishuka.*
202-195	Reign of Emperor Devavarman.*
195-187	Reign of Emperor Shatadhanvan.*
187-184	Reign of Emperor Brihadratha; it ends when he is assassinated by Pushyamitra, one of his generals.*

* Dates of rule and names of the emperors after Ashoka are uncertain—although they are mentioned in several Buddhist texts, the names and dates vary and there is no reliable source.

Chapter One

1. Romila Thapar, *Asoka and the Decline of the Mauryas* (New Delhi: Oxford University Press, 1997), pp. 255-257.
   http://www.scribd.com/doc/31988451/
   Romila-Thapar-Asoka-and-the-Decline-of-the-Mauryas-pp-267-70
2. Charles Masson, *Narrative of Various Journeys in Balochistan, Afghanistan and the Panjab* (London: Richard Bentley, 1842), p. 472.
   http://www.harappa.com/har/masson310.html

Chapter Two

1. Georg Feuerstein, Subhash Kak, and David Frawley, *In Search of the Cradle of Civilization: New Light on Ancient India* (Wheaton, Illinois: Quest Books, 1995), p. 75.
2. Abraham Eraly, *India* (New York: DK Publishing, 2008), p. 235.
3. Ibid., p. 70.

Chapter Three

1. Abraham Eraly, *India* (New York: DK Publishing, 2008), p. 72.
2. Michael Wood, *India* (New York: Basic Books, 2007), p. 71.
3. Alain Daniélou, *A Brief History of India* (Rochester. Vermont: Inner Traditions, 2003), p. 94.
4. Kautilya, "Chapter XIX: The Superintendent of Weights and Measures," *Arthashastra*: Book II: The Duties of Government Superintendents.
   Source Documents and Texts in South Asian Studies, South Dakota State University, Web. 11 Apr. 2010.
   http://www.sdstate.edu/projectsouthasia/upload/Book-II-The-Duties-of-Government-Superintendents.pdf
5. Ibid.
6. Upinder Singh, *A History of Ancient and Early Medieval India: from the Stone Age to the 12th Century* (New Delhi: Pearson Education, 2008), p. 321.
7. Ibid.

Chapter Four

1. Megasthenes, "Of the Manners of the Indians," *Indika,* Fragment XXVII. Strab. XV. i. (53-56, pp. 709-10).
   Source Documents and Texts in South Asian Studies, South Dakota State University, Web. 11 Apr. 2011.
   http://www.sdstate.edu/projectsouthasia/loader.cfm?csModule=security/getfile&PageID=837452

2. Upinder Singh, *A History of Ancient and Early Medieval India: from the Stone Age to the 12th century* (New Delhi: Pearson Education, 2008), p. 325.

3. Megasthenes, "Fragment I or an Epitome of Megasthenes," *Indika,* Fragment I (Diod. II. 36.), Source Documents and Texts in South Asian Studies. South Dakota State University, Web. 11 Apr. 2011. http://www.sdstate.edu/projectsouthasia/loader.cfm?csModule=security/getfile&PageID=837452

4. Kautilya, "Chapter III: The Duty of a Wife.../Concerning Marriage...," *Arthashastra*: Book III: Concerning Law."

    Source Documents and Texts in South Asian Studies. South Dakota State University, Web. 11 Apr. 2011.

    http://www.sdstate.edu/projectsouthasia/upload/Book-III-Concerning-Law.pdf

5. Ibid.

6. Ibid., "Chapter II: Concerning Marriage."

7. Kautilya, "Chapter VII: Restraint of the Organs of Sense—The Life of a Saintly King," Arthashastra: Book I: Concerning Discipline.

    Source Documents and Texts in South Asian Studies, South Dakota State University, Web. 11 Apr. 2011.

    http://www.sdstate.edu/projectsouthasia/upload/Book-I-Concerning-Discipline.pdf

Chapter Five

1. Upinder Singh, *A History of Ancient and Early Medieval India: from the Stone Age to the 12th Century* (New Delhi: Pearson Education, 2008), p. 332.

2. Ibid.

3. Romila Thapar, *Asoka and the Decline of the Mauryas* (New Delhi: Oxford University Press, 1997), p. 250.

    http://www.scribd.com/doc/31988451/Romila-Thapar-Asoka-and-the-Decline-of-the-Mauryas-pp-267-70

4. James Princep, translator, "Edict VII," Ashokan Rock Edicts http://www.sdstate.edu/projectsouthasia/upload/Ashokan-Rock-Edicts-2.pdf

5. Megasthenes, "Of the Manners of the Indians," *Indika*, Fragment XXVII Strab. XV. i. 53-56, pp. 709-10.

    Source Documents and Texts in South Asian Studies, South Dakota State University, Web. 11 Apr. 2011. http://www.sdstate.edu/projectsouthasia/loader.cfm?csModule=security/getfile&PageID=83745

6. Upinder Singh, *A History of Ancient and Early Medieval India,* p. 332.

7. H.G. Wells, *The Outline of History*, (New York: Garden City Publishing, 1929), p. 371.

Books

Daniélou, Alain. *A Brief History of India.* Translated by Kenneth Hurry. Rochester, Vermont: Inner Traditions, 2003.

Das, Sisir Kumar. *History of Indian Literature.* New Delhi: Sahitya Akademi, 2005.

Edwardes, Michael. *A History of India from the Earliest Times to the Present Day.* New York: Farrar, Straus and Cudahy, 1961.

Eraly, Abraham. *India.* New York: DK Publishing, 2008.

Feuerstein, Georg Subhash Kak, and David Frawley. *In Search of the Cradle of Civilization: New Light on Ancient India.* Wheaton, Illinois: Quest Books, 1995.

Kala, Satish Chandra. *Terracottas in the Allahabad Museum.* New Delhi: Abhinav Publications, 1980.

Masson, Charles. *Narrative of various journeys in Balochistan, Afghanistan, the Panjab.* London: Richard Bentley, 1842.

Singh, Upinder. *A History of Ancient and Early Medieval India: From the Stone Age to the 12th Century.* Upper Saddle River, New Jersey: Prentice Hall, 2009.

Thapar, Romila. *Asoka and the Decline of the Mauryas.* New Delhi: Oxford University Press, 1997.

Wells, H.G. *The Outline of History.* New York: Garden City Publishing, 1929.

Wood, Michael. *India.* New York: Basic Books, 2007.

On the Internet

Copper – History and Etymology
http://elements.vanderkrogt.net/element.php?sym=Cu

How to Make Terra Cotta
http://www.ehow.com/how_4829326_make-terra-cotta.html

"Political and Social Organization of the Maurya Empire," *The Cambridge History of India*
http://www.third-millennium-library.com/readinghall/UniversalHistory/INDIA/Cambridge/I/CHAPTER_XIX.html

Source Documents and Texts in South Asian Studies, South Dakota State University
http://www.sdstate.edu/projectsouthasia/Docs/index.cfm

Wilhelm Geiger, translator. "Chapter V: The Third Council," *Mahavamsa: The Great Chronicle of Lanka.*
http://lakdiva.org/mahavamsa/chap005.html

The British Museum, "Silver karshapana of the Maurya Empire."
http://www.britishmuseum.org/explore/highlights/highlight_objects/cm/s/silver_karshapana_of_the_maury.aspx]

Books

Ali, Daud. *Passport to the Past: Ancient India.* New York: Rosen Publishing, 2009.

Apte, Sunita. *India.* Danbury, Connecticut: Children's Press, 2009.

Eraly, Abraham. *India.* New York, N.Y.: DK Publishing, 2008.

Kirsten Holm. *Everyday Life in Ancient India.* New York: PowerKids Press, 2012.

Zamosky, Lisa. *India: World Cultures Through Time.* Huntington Beach, California: Teacher Created Materials, 2008.

On the Internet

The Story of India – PBS
http://www.pbs.org/thestoryofindia/

Buddhism for Kids
http://www.historyforkids.org/learn/india/religion/buddhism.htm

Peacemaker Hero: Ashoka
http://myhero.com/go/hero.asp?hero=Ashoka

Biography of Ashoka the Great
http://asianhistory.about.com/od/india/a/ashoka.htm

Asoka the Great
http://www.iloveindia.com/history/ancient-india/maurya-dynasty/ashoka.html

Mauryan village

ambassador (am-BASS-uh-dohr) - official representative of a foreign government.

assimilation (uh-sihm-uh-LAY-shun) - process by which one group absorbs the culture and practices of another.

ascetic (uh-SEHT-ick) - severe self-discipline; giving up of material comfort.

austerities (aw-STARE-uh-teez)-it- ee) - very simple or without pleasure.

cataclysm (cat-uh-CLIZ-uhm) - large-scale violent upheaval that causes significant destruction.

civilians (suh-VILL-ee-uhnz) - non-soldiers, people not in the military or armed forces.

consolidation (con-sahl-uh-DAY-shun) - the act of uniting or bringing together.

deities (DEE-uh-teez) - gods and goddesses; beings with divine characteristics.

deported (dee-PORE-tuhd) - sent away from existing homes and forced to live somewhere else.

illiterate (il-LIT-uhr-uht) - unable to read or write.

nomadic (no-MAD-ick) - moving from place to place without settling down.

proclamations (praw-cluh-MAY-shuns) - official public announcements.

regal (REE-guhl) - resembling a monarch; magnificent.

reign (RANE) - period of time a person rules.

smelting (SMELL-ting) - to melt or fuse mineral ore.

subsistence (sub-SISS-tunce) – minimum of food and shelter to maintain life.

Tropic of Cancer (TRAW-pick uhv CAN-sehr) - imaginary line that circles the earth about one-fourth of the way between the Equator and the North Pole.

vegetarians (veh-guh-TAHR-ee-uhns) - people who don't eat meat.

PHOTO CREDITS: All photos—CreativeCommons. Every effort has been made to locate all copyright holders of materials used in this book. Any errors or omissions will be corrected in future editions of the book. Recipe on page 40 provided by Salila Sukuman.

Afghanistan 7, 22

Alexander the Great 19, 23, 31

Arthashastra 23–25, 29, 30

Aryans 14

Ashoka 5–7, 33-36

Ashokavadana 34

Bangladesh 7

Bindusara 33, 34

Brihadratha 36

Buddhism 16, 17, 34-36

Cunningham, Sir Alexander 11

Gautama, Siddhartha 17

Harappa 10, 11

Hinduism 14-15, 17

Indika 28-29, 35

Indus River 9,19

Indus Valley 13, 28

Jainism 16, 17, 30

Kalinga 5–6, 34

Kalingaraj 5

Kautilya 21, 24, 33

Khyber Pass 7

Lewis, James (Charles Masson)
    10

Machiavelli, Nicolo 25

Magadha 16, 19

Maurya, Chandragupta 20–24,
    27, 30, 31, 33, 35

Megasthenes 28

Mehrgarh 8

Mohenjo-Daro 10

Muller, Max 13

Nanda, Dhana 22

Nanda, Mahapadma 16

Nepal 7

Nicator, Selecus 20, 22, 28

Pakistan 7-9

Pataliputra 27–28

Pushyamitra 36

Samprati 36

Sarvarthasiddhi 20

Shamashastry, Rudraptnam 25

Sri Lanka 7, 35

Tod, James 31

Vardhamana 17

Vedas (Four) 14

Wells, H.G. 36